Exploring Materials

Paper

Abby Colich

Heinemann
LIBRARY
Chicago, Illinois

Edited by Abby Colich, Daniel Nunn, and Catherine Veitch
Designed by Marcus Bell
Picture research by Tracy Cummins
Production by Victoria Fitzgerald
Originated by Capstone Global Library Ltd
Printed in the United States of America in
North Mankato, Minnesota. 052015 008946RP

Library of Congress Cataloging-in-Publication Data
Colich, Abby.
  Paper / Abby Colich.
    pages cm.—(Exploring materials)
  Includes bibliographical references and index.
  ISBN 978-1-4329-8016-0 (hb)—ISBN 978-1-4329-8024-5 (pb) 1.
Paper—Juvenile literature. I. Title.

TS1105.5.C65 2014
676—dc23   2012047491

Acknowledgments
The author and publisher are grateful to the following for permission to reproduce copyright material: Corbis p. 11 (© Imaginechina); Getty Images pp. 4 (© Bonita Cooke), 8 (© moodboard), 10, 23c (© Dev Carr), 15, 23a (© Lonely Planet), 19 (© Alistair Berg); Istockphoto p. 7 (© ei); Photo Researchers, Inc pp. 9 inset, 23b (© Tommaso Guicciardini); Shutterstock pp. 5 (© Subbotina Anna), 6a (© luchunyu), 6b (© Daniel Korzeniewski), 6c (© Ruth Black), 6d (© modd), 12 (© kotomiti), 13 (© AISPIX by Image Source), 14 (© Anatoliy Samara), 16 (© Zulhazmi Zabri), 17 (© Juriah Mosin), 18 (© Fer Gregory), 20 (© oznyakov), 22 (© Marcie Fowler - Shining Hope Images, © photobank.ch, © Elena Schweitzer); Superstock pp. 9, 23b (© John Zoiner/age fotostock), 21 (© age fotostock).

Cover photograph of a boy holding cut-out figures reproduced with permission of Superstock (© Juice Images). Back cover photograph reproduced with permission of Shutterstock (© kotomiti).

We would like to thank Valarie Akerson, Nancy Harris, Dee Reid, and Diana Bentley for their invaluable help in the preparation of this book.

Every effort has been made to contact copyright holders of any material reproduced in this book. Any omissions will be rectified in subsequent printings if notice is given to the publisher.

Contents

What Is Paper?

Paper is a material.

Materials are what things are made from.

We use paper to make many different things.

Paper has many uses.

Where Does Paper Come From?

Paper comes from trees or other plants.

pulp

Wood is cut up and made into a pulp. The pulp is made into paper.

Paper can be recycled or reused.

Recycled paper can be used to make new things.

What Is Paper Like?

Paper can be different colors.

thin

thick

Paper can be thin or thick.
Thick paper is called cardboard.

Paper can be cut and folded.

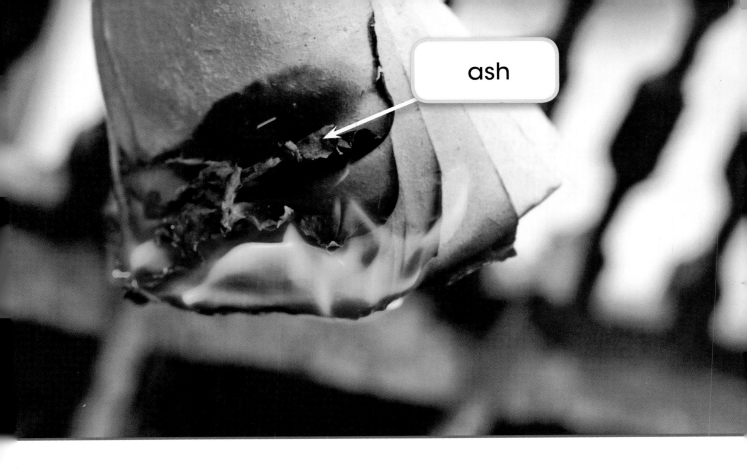

ash

Paper can burn and turn into ash.

How Do We Use Paper?

We use paper to share stories.

We use paper to write letters.

We use paper to wrap foods
and drinks.

We use paper to store and carry things.

We use paper to paint on.

We use paper to blow our noses!

Quiz

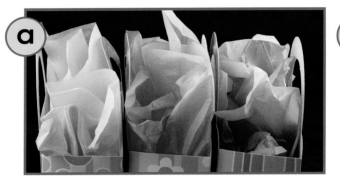

a

b

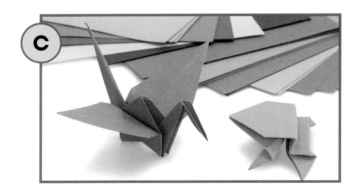

c

Which of these things are made from paper?

Answer on page 24.

Picture Glossary

 **ash** gray powder left behind after something is burned. Burned paper turns into ash.

 **pulp** mixture of ground-up wood and water

 **recycle** make used items into new things

Index

The **tissue paper (a)** and **colored paper (c)** are made from paper.

Notes for Parents and Teachers
Before reading
Ask children if they have heard the term "material" and what they think it means. Reinforce the concept of materials. Explain that all objects are made from different materials. A material is something that takes up space and can be used to make other things. Ask children to give examples of different materials. These may include glass, plastic, and paper.

To get children interested in the topic, ask if they know what paper is. Identify any misconceptions they may have. Ask them to think about whether their ideas might change as the book is read.

After reading
- Check to see if any of the identified misconceptions have changed.
- Show the children examples of paper, including newspapers, books, and cardboard.
- Pass the paper objects around. Ask the children to describe the properties of each item. Is the paper heavy or light? Is it thick or thin? Can it bend and fold? Ask them to name other items made from paper.